The Baseball Reporter

by Ted Fashum

Illustrated by Stacey Schuett

For as long as he could remember, Anton's favorite sport was baseball. He would dream about it at night. In his dreams, he was a star; he was called the next Ernie Banks. In his dreams, he was getting in the Hall of Fame. He wanted to be the best baseball player ever.

Anton played baseball whenever he could since he wanted to improve his game. In spring and summer, he and his friends played ball in the park. In winter, he and his friends played inside. They pitched balls and took turns at bat. They bunted and hit fly balls. All of his friends seemed to be getting better. Anton wasn't getting better.

Anton liked playing, but he made mistakes. At bat, Anton could not hit the ball far or hard. Once the ball even hit him. In the field, he could not catch flies, and he dropped balls that were grounded to him. He just could not keep the ball in his hands. At base, he couldn't catch the ball or tag the runners if he did catch it.

Anton was not good at the game of baseball. This upset Anton and frustrated his coach.

Anton didn't like how he was playing and went to talk to the coach. "I know I'm not very good," he moaned. "But what can I do to get better?"

"I suspect this is not the game for you, but I know how much you like baseball. I will help you find a way to stay with the team," said the coach.

"What else can I do?" Anton asked. "I really like baseball. I want to be part of the team and involved in the game."

The coach said to Anton, "There are lots of ways to be part of our team and stay involved in the game of baseball. You could manage the equipment and help me with the batting lineup. You could also compile the stats for each player after the games."

Anton wondered if he could stay in baseball but not play. It would be hard to sit on the side and watch his friends play without him.

6

At the next home game, Anton took notes. He listed the team members and what they did. He used his notes to write a story. He double-checked his notes to make sure the story was correct and then he sent it to the local newspaper. To his surprise, they liked it and published his story!

His friends called him when they saw the story with his name on it. "You may not play ball well, but you sure know how to write about it," they said.

Today you will see Anton on the five o'clock news. He is sitting in the TV booth. He does the play by play. You can listen to him tell what happens in the game. You can look at the replays.

On the show, Anton talks about the home team winning the pennant. He tells stories about the unsung heroes of the game. Tune him in, and you will find out how much he likes the game. You will see that he has become a star and baseball expert.